Mountain Animals

Mountain Animals

17 68

ENCYCLOPÆDIA BRITANNICA

CHICAGO•LONDON•TORONTO•GENEVA•SYDNEY•TOKYO•MANILA•SEOUL

Advisory Board

The Treasury of American Wildlife advisory board was established to help make this book series a unique effort toward further understanding of our wildlife resources. Members come from many walks of life and share a common interest in preserving America's priceless wildlife heritage.

ISBN: 0-85229-370-4   © **1979 by Encyclopaedia Britannica, Inc.**   Printed in U.S.A.

Table of Contents

The Mountains 6

The Grizzly Bear 9

The Mountain Goat 17

The Mountain Lion 25

The Golden Eagle 31

The Hoary Marmot 37

The Rainbow Trout 43

The Bighorn Sheep 49

The Clark's Nutcracker .. 57

What Can YOU Do? 62

The Mountains

America has two major mountain ranges—the Appalachians of the East and the rugged Rockies of the West. The wildlife described in this book lives in the Rockies.

These creatures spend short but glorious summers in high country, many above the tree line. There's an abundance of fresh food as snow melts away to a carpet of wildflowers. Bighorn sheep graze in alpine meadows while golden eagles soar overhead. Mountain goats stand stiff-legged on the highest ledges.

Mountain creatures give birth and raise their young quickly in high country. The first snowfall sends most of them down to the shelter and food of forests and alpine glades.

Winter in the Rockies can be fierce. Bears crawl into dens for the winter. Hoary marmots spend the winter in deep sleep. Nature equipped other animals to survive winter. Sheep and goats have special hooves to help them walk on slippery rocks and narrow ledges. Some birds and animals turn white in winter to blend with the snowy landscape.

Wildlife of the Rocky Mountains are a spendid group of creatures. They live in one of the most beautiful and breathtaking areas of our continent.

America's Mountains

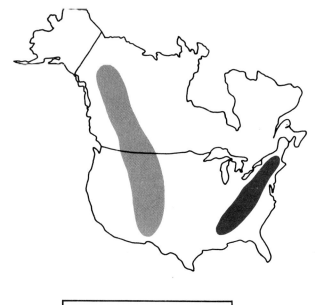

☐	Rocky Mountains
■	Appalachian Mountains

Alpine Meadow

Grizzly Bear

This huge creature lives in the most remote areas of the mountains. Man is its enemy and has almost eliminated it. Bears fish, eat berries and many other foods.

Mountain Goat

No other animal is more skilled in climbing cliffs and ledges. The mountain goat lives above most of its enemies. It has very keen sight and hearing. Goats eat grasses and herbs.

Mountain Lion

The mountain lion ranged over most of North America before man came. Now it is found only in lonely mountain country. The lion hunts the wildlife of its area.

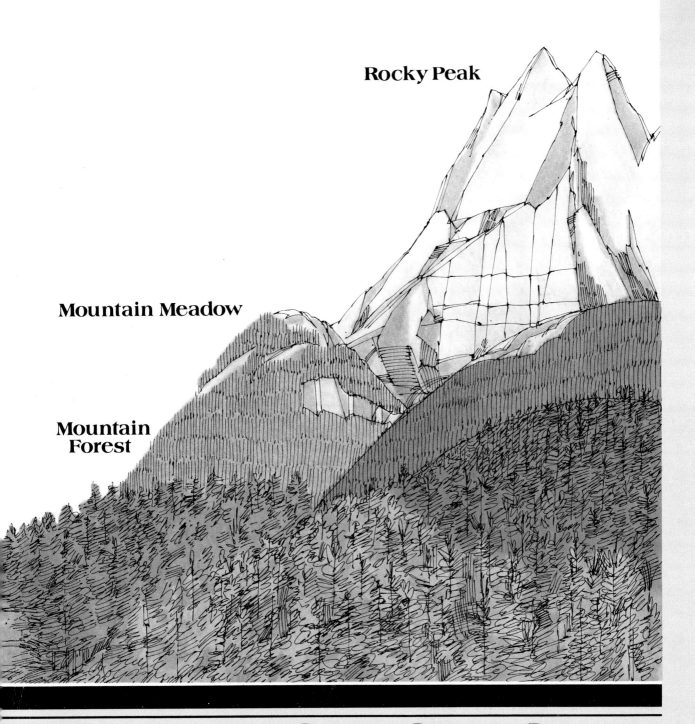

Rocky Peak

Mountain Meadow

Mountain Forest

Golden Eagle

This great bird nests high in the mountains. Its wide wings help the eagle soar on rising air currents. This eagle prefers marmots, also eats ground squirrels and rodents.

Hoary Marmot

This shy creature lives above the tree line. During the summer, the marmot stuffs itself with fresh alpine grasses. The other months are spent sleeping in its tunnel den.

Rainbow Trout

Clear, cold mountain streams are the home of this popular game fish. Trout swim upstream to spawn, often through cascading rapids. Insects and larvae are favorite foods.

Bighorn Sheep

This agile sheep likes high mountains. It grazes the lush grasses of the alpine meadows in summer and lower pastures in winter.

Clark's Nutcracker

This bird is well-known as the roadside beggar of the West. It is a gray bird with black and white wings. You'll find it in the high mountains.

The Grizzly Bear

Of all the ferocious animals in North America, the grizzly bear is one of the most savage and most feared. One swipe of its huge paw is enough to kill an animal or even a man.

The bear's scientific name is *Ursus horribilis*, and horrible it can be. The name "grizzly" refers to the grizzled look it gets from the silver-tipped guard hairs that cover its black, brown or yellow coat. The hump on the bear's back makes it look even more threatening.

In the days of the pioneers, the largest of all grizzlies, the Plains grizzly, fed on the huge herds of bison that covered the prairies. The Plains grizzly sent such famous explorers as Lewis and Clark, Kit Carson and Wild Bill Hickok scurrying for safety. Later, settlers with guns and poisons did everything they could to destroy the Plains grizzly. They succeeded, and now that particular species of grizzly is gone forever.

In fact, today nearly all the grizzlies that lived throughout the West are gone. There are only about 1,000 of the great bears left in the lower 48 states. They are found in wilderness regions in and around Glacier and Yellowstone National Parks, plus a small area on the northern borders of Idaho and Montana. Fortunately, many more grizzlies still live in Canada and Alaska.

Bad eating habits

The grizzly bear's biggest problem seems to be its appetite. Though considered a carnivore, or eater of flesh, the grizzly, like other bears, eats almost anything. It grazes on grass, eats leaves, fruit, berries and other wild plants. It hunts rodents, such as ground squir-

rels, often digging them out of their dens with its four inch (10 centimeter) long front claws. Grizzlies also eat many other small mammals, lizards, insects and fish. The big bears love to catch salmon as the fish migrate up northern rivers.

The bear's appetite becomes

open when they are away. They save themselves the trouble of replacing locked doors that the bears tear open.

The worst problem, however, has to do with the grizzly's fondness for garbage. In national parks, great numbers of grizzlies began to invade campground dumps in search of scraps. The Park Service finally closed the dumps and built bear-proof garbage cans in the early 1970s. Unfortunately, this made the problem worse for a while, because the grizzlies had grown used to scavenging for human food. When this easy supply of food disappeared, the hungry bears began to harass tourists and campers. Many people were injured, and a few were killed.

The most recent problem with grizzly bears is that many of them seem to be losing their fear of people. The powerful bears are now attacking people who pack food into remote camping sites. Female grizzlies will attack anyone who gets too close to their cubs. There seems to be no solution to this latest problem, other than to reserve some of the parks for the bears.

a problem when it goes after humans' food. In some areas cattle have replaced the grizzly's natural food. Hungry bears will kill and eat cattle when they have the opportunity. This, of course, upsets ranchers. Another of the grizzly's bad habits is to raid cabins containing supplies of food. In some areas, cabin owners leave their doors

Native Americans called it "brother"

The Plains Indians had so much respect for the grizzly that they called it "brother." They believed that the bear was related to them. It could walk upright, hold things in its paws and, after it was skinned, it looked like a human. Any brave who killed a grizzly was honored more than a brave who killed a human enemy. When a grizzly was killed, its skull was stuck on a pole and taken to a holy place, where the Indians believed the spirit of the dead bear would be happy.

Sign of the grizzly

To find out if grizzly bears inhabit an area, all you have to do is read the signs. Look for tracks. The long claws on the grizzly's front feet make marks that are unlike those of any other animal in the North American wilderness. Grizzly bears follow the same trails for generations. The bears will even place their feet in the exact paw prints made by the many bears that walked there before. These trails are so heavily used that they become "bear highways." The wide, twin ruts worn by the bears have grass between them and look like ruts made by cars.

Another sign of the grizzly is the mark it makes on certain trees. With its long front claws, the bear scratches as high up as it can reach to make marks on the trunks of "bear trees." Bear trees are apparently used by many generations of bears and may be a warning to other grizzlies to stay out. Other bear trees are used by grizzlies to scratch themselves. When winter coats are being shed during the spring, the bears' habit of scratching off the itchy, loose hair makes rub marks on the trees.

When the bear digs out ground squirrels from their dens, it moves great amounts of earth. This is still another sign of the grizzly—no other animal in the forest digs that much.

It's a cub's life

Grizzly bears mate in late spring and early summer. It is not known if a boar, or male, mates with more than one sow, or female, but the parent bears do spend several weeks together and then never see each other again.

The cubs, usually two, are born in January when the sow is in her winter den. The newborn cubs weigh about 1½ pounds (680 grams) and are eight to nine inches (20 to 23 centimeters) long. At birth, the cubs are covered with short gray hair, and their eyes are sealed shut. The sow licks her newborns clean and dry and then cuddles them close so that they can take her milk. The sow probably sleeps on and off for the rest of the winter.

The cubs grow and develop as they are nourished by their mother's milk. By the time the family leaves the den in late April, the cubs have matured enough to follow their mother as she searches for food. By midsummer, the youngsters are able to eat the mice and ground squirrels the sow catches and by fall, they are no longer taking her milk. The cubs still will den up with their mother during their second winter and for this reason, female grizzlies only raise a family of cubs every two or three years.

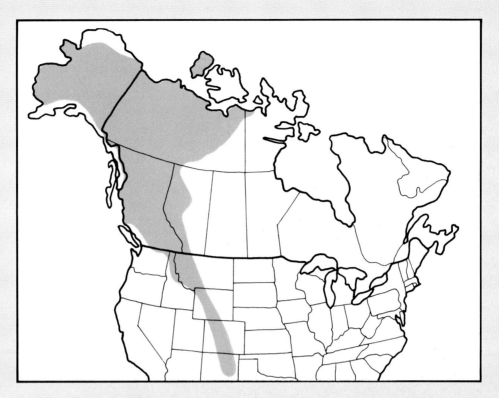

GRIZZLY BEAR FACTS

Habitat: Wilderness areas and high mountains of the West and the tundra of the far North.

Habits: Most active in early morning and evening, but may be out any time of the day or night; usually alone or in small family groups. Hibernates in north country and in high mountains during winter; uses same trails over and over again.

Food: Eats most anything: meat, fish, fruits, grasses and insects.

Size and Weight: Head and body six-eight feet (2-2½ meters); height at shoulders 3-3½ feet (0.9-1.1 meters); 325-850 pounds (147-386 kilograms); four inch (10 centimeter) claws on front feet.

Life Span: Twenty-five years or more.

Locomotion: Can walk upright like a human. Moves very fast, but also walks, trots, gallops and swims well.

Voice: Growls, whines, snorts, bawls and roars. Cubs cry if separated from their mother.

The Mountain Goat

The highest and most dangerous ledges of our northwestern mountains are home to the mountain goat. For this reason, the goat is relatively safe from its enemies, including humans.

The mountain goat is not really a goat. In fact, it's a kind of antelope. There are no other animals like it in North America. Its closest relatives are the tahr and serow of Asia and the chamois of Europe. It is believed that the mountain goat originated in Asia and came to North America more than a half million years ago across the Bering Land Bridge, which once connected Siberia and Alaska.

Because its home is so difficult for humans to reach, very little was known about the mountain goat until quite recently. Indeed, the first record of the creature was incorrect. It came from the diary of Captain James Cook in 1778. When the Indians showed Cook the white animals high on the mountain, he called them polar bears.

Such mistakes are still made today. When tourists spot mountain goats on the high, sheer cliffs of Glacier National Park in Montana, they often call them bighorn sheep.

In the early 1800s, naturalist Alexander Henry was the first to describe the mountain goat correctly: "The white goat is larger than the gray sheep (bighorn), thickly covered with long, pure white wool and has short, black, neatly erect horns," he wrote. "These animals seldom leave the mountain tops. Winter and summer they prefer the highest regions."

Super mountain climber

Like Arctic animals, which also live in cold and snowy areas, the mountain goat's thick white coat and special footgear are well-suited to its high mountain home. In fact, it is the most sure-footed of all hoofed animals on this continent. There are few mountains that the goat cannot climb. When threatened, it merely heads for the highest and most dangerous rocks. For millions of years, goats have been able to escape their enemies in this way. The golden eagle is the only enemy they

cannot escape, because it can fly into those high places. Occasionally, an eagle will swoop down and steal a young goat off the rocks.

Mountain goats have special equipment for climbing. On the bottom of each half of the goat's hoof is a thick cup of tough skin. When the goats climb up or down, the cups form a suction on the rocks. The goat's superb sense of balance also helps. When climbing, it seems almost to fly from one ledge to another. A miss would mean sure death, but if the goat runs out of room on the ledge, it does not panic. Instantly, it decides what to do next. This may mean rising up on its hind feet, turning all the way around and going back the way it came. When climbing to a higher ledge, the goat uses its front feet to pull itself up, the way a man uses his arms.

Surprisingly, the goat is not a good broad jumper. Six feet (two meters) across is about all it can manage. It can do much better when jumping down.

Some goats do slip and fall to their deaths, but rock and snow slides are a greater danger. In fact more die this way than from attacks by enemies.

Good eyes and ears

The mountain goat's sense of smell is good, but not as good as its hearing and sight. Both are well developed because the goat depends on them as a warning system against enemies. Goats must train themselves to learn the difference between the noise of rocks falling naturally and the sound of rocks tumbling in the wake of an approaching enemy.

The goat's eyesight is outstanding. It lives far above most of its enemies, and it can see movement at great distances. A hunter approaching from below will almost always be seen in time for the goat to escape. For some reason, however, the goat is not as wary of movement from above. It can be fooled much more easily by a hunter who approaches from a higher ledge or cliff.

Small but dangerous horns

Both male and female mountain goats have permanent horns that start to grow from birth and get bigger every year. By the first winter of a young goat's life, its horns will be about three inches (7½ centimeters) long. During the winter, when food is scarce, the horn grows more slowly and forms only a narrow ridge or ring. By counting the rings, one can tell how many winters the goat has lived. With luck, mountain goats survive 12 to 15 winters.

Compared to other animals' horns, a mountain goat's horns are short, but very sharp. A big billy, or male, may have horns

only 12 inches (30 centimeters) long. The nanny's, or female's, seldom are more than nine inches (22½ centimeters). Nannys use their horns to protect their young, called kids, against enemies. Billys use them in fierce fights with other males for the attention of the females in the herd. It's not unusual for some billys to die of wounds they receive in these battles.

Billys have harems, or herds, of several nannys. It is believed that billys wander from one group of nannys and kids to another during the October and November breeding season.

No place for a kid

This dangerous world of steep cliffs and high ledges may not seem like the best place for a baby animal, but mountain goat kids do survive. They are born in April or May. The female usually chooses a private, protected area on the mountain in which to give birth. Within a few minutes after birth, the seven to eight pound (2½ to three kilogram) youngster is standing and taking milk from its mother. In half an hour, the kid is stiffly hopping about, trying out its legs. The nanny usually keeps it hidden in the rocks for a couple of days, returning every two hours or so to feed it. By the end of the kid's

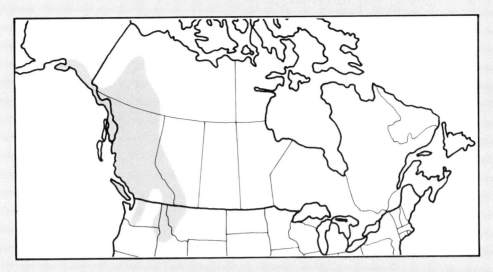

MOUNTAIN GOAT FACTS

Habitat: Rocky ledges and steep slopes at or above timberlines of the northwestern mountains.

Habits: Live in groups of fewer than 30; active during daylight; billys have harems and wander from one nanny and kid group to another; both males and females have horns.

Food: Grasses and herbs of the high mountain country.

Size and Weight: Average 100-200 pounds (37-75 kilograms), some males over 300 pounds (136 kilograms); 60-70 inches (1.5-1.75 meters) long; 40 inches (one meter) high; at birth seven-eight pounds (2½-3 kilograms) and 13 inches (0.3 meters) high.

Life Span: Twelve to 15 years.

Locomotion: Stiff-legged walk; seldom run; exceptional sense of balance; good at climbing but can broad jump only about six feet (two meters).

Voice: Quiet, except for occasional grunts and snorts; kids bleat and hum.

first week, it has joined the other goats.

Soon the youngster begins to nibble at different kinds of plants it sees its mother eating. It spends much of its first summer playing, dashing and bounding with other kids over the dangerous rocks and cliffs. The young goats seem to get a special thrill out of rushing up to the very edge of a steep cliff, stopping just in time not to fall.

The kid stays with the nanny for about two years. The mother probably stays with her youngster longer than most animals do because of the many dangerous places in the high mountains where they live.

The Mountain Lion

Imagine what a house cat would be like if it had been raised in the wild, learned to hunt for its own food and to fight for its life against fierce enemies. Then picture the same wild cat, 30 times the size of a pet cat. That's a mountain lion!

The mountain lion's range once covered an area greater than that of any other land mammal in our hemisphere. The cat's territory stretched from the northernmost areas of Canada to the very tip of South America, and from the Atlantic coast to the Pacific. When white people came to North America, the mountain lion was pushed out of the eastern states and was forced to move farther and farther west. Today, the cats are still found from Canada to South America, but in greatly reduced numbers.

Since the days of our earliest settlers, the mountain lion has been hunted without mercy. The big cat is a fresh meat eater, preferring deer meat to all other food. But occasionally, when game is scarce, or when a mountain lion is old and weak, or young and inexperienced as a hunter, it will kill domestic livestock. Early ranchers who lost cows, sheep and horses to mountain lions declared all-out war on the cats. In most states, bounties, or rewards of money, were paid for every mountain lion killed. Practices such as this all but wiped out the mountain lion in the United States. Today, all states have stopped paying bounties. The mountain lion is now considered a game animal and as such is given special protection. Where lion hunting seasons are still held, they are carefully controlled.

A mountain lion is a puma is a cougar is a...

Because the mountain lion's range extended over such a vast area, it was known by many different names. In the English language alone, there are 42 names for the cat. If we add the names given to it by the Spanish and the Indians, the number would be well over 100. Some of the more common names are cougar, puma, panther, catamount, painter and American lion. The mountain lion's scientific name is *Felis concolor*. *Felis* means "cat," and *concolor* means "of one color."

A skilled hunter

Deer are the mountain lion's staff of life. The animals taken by the mountain lion tend to be old, weak or sick. The cat, by eliminating unfit deer, keeps the remaining herd healthy and strong.

The mountain lion hunts by sneaking up on its victim. Moving noiselessly on soft, padded feet, the cat crouches low to the ground and creeps as close to the deer as it dares without scaring it. Then, tail twitching, feet drawn under its body, claws gripping the soil, the cat springs forward. The motions it goes through are the same as those of a pet cat pouncing on a mouse or plaything.

Usually, the pounce is forceful enough to knock the animal off its feet. Instantly, the cat sinks its sharp teeth into the prey's neck. One set of claws tears into the animal's back while the other jerks the head backward, often breaking the neck. Death is quick.

After the kill has been made the lion drags its dinner to nearby cover. Some mountain lions are strong enough to drag a 900 pound (405 kilogram) moose a distance of 300 feet (91 meters). Seven or eight pounds (2½ or three kilograms) of meat is enough to satisfy the lion's appetite, so if there is meat left over, the lion covers it with leaves or snow. It will return to the kill for more feeding until the meat begins to spoil.

Though the mountain lion enjoys deer meat above all others, it will hunt a variety of game. On rare occasions, it may take an elk or a moose. More often, it will feed on porcupines, rabbits, hares and other rodents, including mice. The mighty cat will even eat grasshoppers.

Kittenhood

Mountain lions are loners for most of their lives, but a mated pair stays together for a few weeks to breed. There is no breeding season among mountain lions. They may mate at any time of the year, though breeding usually seems to occur between December and March.

Three months later, the female delivers her litter. The young, called kittens or cubs, are born in a well-hidden den.

The den may be a cave, a deep separation in the rocks or under a rocky ledge that provides good cover. There may be from one to six kittens, but two or three is most common. They are covered with short, soft, buff-colored fur with distinct black spots on the body and rings around the tail. At birth, they weigh from one-half to one pound (227 to 454 grams) and are about 10 inches (25 centimeters) long. The newborn kittens' eyes are sealed shut until they are about 10 days old.

Until their eyes open, the kittens do little more than sleep and drink their mother's milk. But by the time they are two weeks old, they are active and playful.

When the kittens are a month old, their mother starts to bring them bits of meat. During the next month, she will make a kill, return to the den and lead the kittens back to it. At six months, they will make their first awkward attempts at hunting.

The wild kittens are much the same as domestic kittens. They play the same kinds of games, creeping up and pouncing on each other's tails—or their mother's. Like a domestic mother cat, a mother mountain lion is very patient with her little rascals.

The kittens gain about a pound (454 grams) a week until they are nearly full grown. The spots on their coat fade as they grow, usually disappearing by the time the youngsters are six months old. The mother keeps her cubs with her until they are at least a year old, sometimes longer. They are almost full grown by this time, but young mountain lions will not begin to raise a family until they are two to three years old.

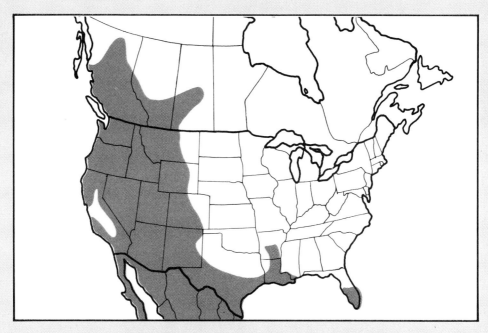

MOUNTAIN LION FACTS

Habitat: Rugged mountains and hilly woodlands of western United States.

Habits: Secretive; few are ever seen in the wild. Spends most of its life alone. Mixes with others only as a youngster or for short periods in adulthood during mating season.

Food: Favorite food is deer. Also eats rabbits, porcupine, hare and other rodents; occasionally it will take an elk. Rarely, domestic livestock.

Size and Weight: Measures 7-9½ feet (two-three meters) from nose to tip of tail. Weights vary from 80-275 pounds (36-125 kilograms). Females are about one-third smaller than males.

Life Span: Probably 12 years. Some known to live in the wild for at least 18 years.

Locomotion: Walks in long strides, gallops, leaps. Climbs trees well. Prefers to stay away from water, but is a good swimmer.

Voice: Rarely makes noises, but has all the same notes as a domestic cat. It mews, purrs, spits, hisses and screams, but much louder.

The mountain screamer

"Mountain screamer" is one of the many names by which the mountain lion is known. Though it rarely makes any sound at all, the mountain lion is known for a scream that can make your hair stand on end. Most of the screeches that are thought to come from mountain lions can be traced to barn owls or other creatures. But every once in awhile, prob-ably when it is looking for a mate, the lion will make an unforgettable sound. Very few people have heard it, but those who have agree that it sounds like the scream of a terrified woman. Under the right condi-tions, it can be heard for at least a mile (1.6 kilometers).

Mountain lions also make other sounds of domestic cats.

The Golden Eagle

The golden eagle makes its home high above the grassy prairie on rugged ledges of rocky cliffs. The 70 square miles (180 square kilometers) surrounding this lookout and nesting place is a male eagle's domain, or territory. He is called a tiercel, and his mate, the hen.

The golden eagle feeds on rabbits, ground squirrels, mice and moles. It also eats many kinds of birds, raccoons, weasels, even skunks and porcupines. Unlike the bald eagle, which survives largely on dead fish, the golden eagle preys on live animals. This swift hunter strikes down its victim with the full force of its heavy body, and sharp claws quickly complete the kill.

Occasionally, a golden eagle may feed on a dead animal. A bird found eating a dead lamb may not have killed it, but sheep ranchers are likely to believe otherwise. Because of their exaggerated reputation for killing range animals, thousands of golden eagles have been shot needlessly. Hunting them from an airplane or helicopter is considered sport by some ranchers, but both golden and bald eagles are protected by law. Hunting them from planes violates the federal Airborne Hunting Act.

The golden eagle is more plentiful than the bald eagle, but numbers still are very small. Now, they are most often found in remote mountain areas.

How to identify a golden eagle

The golden eagle and the bald eagle (which is our national bird) are the largest American birds of prey except for the California condor. An adult golden eagle weighs from eight to 13 pounds (three to five kilograms). From tip to tip, its wings will spread seven feet (two meters) or more.

Golden eagles are very dark brown in color and look black at a distance. The name "golden" comes from the golden brown feathers on the bird's head and neck. Legs are feathered to the toes. Plains Indians valued the golden eagle's feathers for headdresses to wear at their tribal ceremonies.

You may mistake an adult golden eagle for a young bald eagle. Bald eagles do not have a white head and tail until they are three or four years old. Mistakes are not common, since the two birds usually live in different habitats, but they do sometimes migrate together. If you see these eagles in flight, the white in the wing linings of the young bald eagle will help you to tell the difference between the two. The wing linings of the older golden eagle are always dark.

Eagles may live to be 25 to 30 years old if unharmed by humans. A pair will remain mated for life, but at the death of one, the surviving golden eagle will find a new mate.

An old folk tale

Long ago, people used to think that eagles could carry off young children. Today we know this is impossible. Scientists have learned that an adult 11 pound (four kilogram) golden eagle cannot rise from the ground with more than five pounds (two kilograms) of weight clutched in its claws.

The eagle's eyrie

The huge nests of both golden and bald eagles are called "eyries." Most bald eagles build their nests in treetops. Golden eagles sometimes nest in trees. Usually they choose a rocky ledge high on a steep cliff. The eyrie is a large mass of sticks and roots, lined with grass, leaves and mosses, and measures as much as six to eight feet (two to three meters) in diameter.

Eggs and young

The female lays two eggs, sometimes one, rarely three. She starts to incubate immediately after the first egg is laid, and two or three days go by before she lays her second egg. As a result, the first egg hatches before the others, and the baby from that egg is always larger than the rest until they all reach their full growth.

One egg may be almost pure white, but more often the eggs are dull white or cream-colored, beautifully marked with shades of brown and purple. Before golden eagles were protected by law, egg collectors looked for these eggs to add to their exhibits.

The hen sits on the eggs for over a month. The tiercel usually does not help incubate, but he brings food to his mate during her long wait for the eggs to hatch. He also helps bring food to the young.

Newly hatched eaglets are covered with white down. They are fed in the nest by the parent birds for nine to 10 weeks. Even after they learn to fly, the young remain near the nest for a long time.

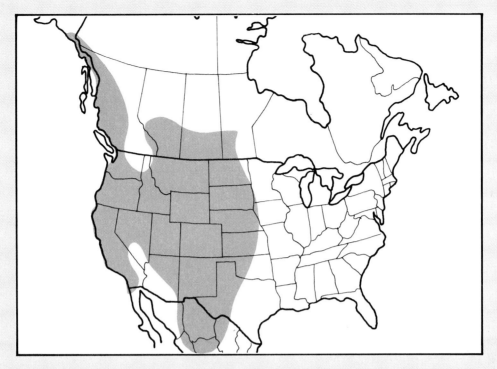

GOLDEN EAGLE FACTS
Habitat: Mountains and badlands of the West.
Habits: Usually lives where found, but some migrate in autumn, especially in East. Mate for life.
Food: Rabbits, marmots, ground squirrels, mice, moles and birds, taken alive by swift, winged pursuit.
Size and Weight: Thirty to 40 inches (75-103 centimeters) long; wingspread 6⅓-7⅔ feet (2-2½ meters). Weight, adult male, about nine pounds (4 kilograms); females, 12 pounds (5.5 kilograms).
Life Span: If they survive their first year, they may live to be 20 or more.
Locomotion: Powerful and majestic flyer.
Voice: Mostly silent but may emit a series of high-pitched squeals or whistles.

Golden eagles rare in the East

Most of the golden eagles in our country soar over the western mountains and prairies. They are rarely found east of the Mississippi River, although long ago the golden eagle was known to nest in the mountains of New England. Even today, some of these majestic birds are seen each autumn at Hawk Mountain in eastern Pennsylvania as they glide south on the air currents from some northern wilderness where they still may nest. A shortage of food far to the north may account for the fall migration of golden eagles along the eastern ridges.

The Hoary Marmot

High in the mountains, too high for trees to grow, lives an animal few people see. It is the hoary marmot, a large relative of the woodchuck, and it lives in the most northern and western North American mountains. Its cousin, the yellow-bellied marmot, also is found on mountaintops, but it lives farther south in the United States than the hoary and can also be seen in western valleys and foothills. Both marmots belong to the same family as prairie dogs and squirrels.

The hoary marmot makes its home in rock slides and slopes where it can hide from its enemies under and between rocks. Sometimes it uses a high rock as a sunning place and lookout spot. If disturbed, it sounds a whistling signal before scurrying to its burrow. The burrow may be 20 feet (six meters) long and have several exits. The marmot's nest is lined with grass and hair to keep out cold during the winter months.

The animal's warm fur coat is grayish black underneath, with white-tipped guard hairs. Its head and shoulders are patterned in black and white, and its feet have black "boots." Hoary marmots grow to be about twice as big as woodchucks.

On summer days these playful, sociable animals leave their burrows to eat and to enjoy the sun. They prefer herbaceous (not woody) green plants of the alpine meadow, including flowers, wild onion and lettuce, berries, roots, grasses, seeds and grains.

The whistler

Long ago, French fur traders in Canada called the hoary marmot *le siffleur*. In English, this means "the whistler." It's a good name, because the marmot's shrill warning whistle is so loud that on a calm day, it can be heard a mile (1.6 kilometers) away.

Food of the high mountain predators

Hoary marmots are the food of many four-footed animals—wolves, coyotes, foxes and lynxes. Even a grizzly bear may dig a marmot out of its burrow, and marmots are the golden eagle's favorite food. It's a vital link in the food chain.

The short summers

In late spring, after hibernating for as long as nine months, the hoary marmot sleepily stumbles from its den. To reach the sunlight, it may have tunneled several feet through snow. In spite of a long winter without food, it does not eat right away and seems to take little interest in its surroundings. But as the weather grows warmer, snow melts and plants sprout new green shoots, the marmot begins to revive. Before long, it is stuffing itself with fresh green plants and looking for a mate.

Summer is short, and the period between mating and birth of the marmot's young is also brief, usually about a month to six weeks. Four or five babies are born in a fresh, rebuilt nest in the burrow, and the newborns stay close to their mother all summer. She provides them with milk for about 40 days, and by the end of the summer, they are able to care for themselves. The young marmots will not have babies of their own until they are two years old.

By September, it is time for

MH Country School

the animals to prepare for hibernation. Some biologists believe the youngsters spend their first winter hibernating with their mother in the home nest.

The long winters

As the days get shorter and colder, the marmot prepares a warm nest and eats almost to the bursting point. The food is stored in its body as a special kind of fat, called brown fat, which provides enough energy for the animal to survive the long winter without eating.

When a marmot is ready to hibernate, it curls up into a fuzzy ball in its nest. This protects its belly, where the fur is thinnest. The ball shape, used by most animals for hibernating, exposes the least possible surface to the cold.

The marmot does not "go to sleep" all at once. Instead, its body slows down in stages, reawakening several times. With each stage, its body temperature drops lower until it reaches the temperature of the surrounding nest, usually about 45 or 50 degrees Fahrenheit (seven or 10 degrees Celsius). By then it is breathing only three times a minute, so lightly you cannot even see it take a breath. Its heart is beating very, very slowly. The marmot is so near death that it does not react if it is touched or picked up.

During this period of so-called sleep, when the animal cannot be awakened, the marmot's body is barely functioning and needs very little nourishment. Even so, about 40 percent of its body weight is lost during hibernation. After such a winter, it is no wonder the hoary marmot is groggy when it finally makes its way from its den.

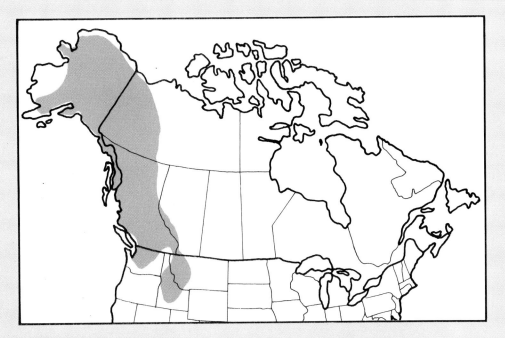

HOARY MARMOT FACTS
Habitat: Rocky slopes and alpine meadows of high western mountains.
Habits: Active during daylight; lives in family groups; has long period of hibernation.
Food: Flowering plants, berries, roots, grasses, seeds, grains.
Size and Weight: Length: tip of nose to base of tail, 18-21 inches (45-53 centimeters); tail 7-10 inches (18-25 centimeters); weight, 8-20 pounds (3½-9 kilograms).
Life Span: Up to 10 years.
Locomotion: Runs on short legs.
Voice: Shrill whistle.

What good is a hoary marmot?

The hoary marmot is not of great value to humans, either as food or for fur. On the other hand, it does not interfere in any way with human activities. Its place in the world is chiefly to provide food for the meat eaters of the high mountains.

The Rainbow Trout

To find a rainbow trout, look for the invisible fish in invisible water. Trout live in cold, clean streams so sparkling clear that the bottom of quiet pools can be seen almost as clearly as if the water were glass. The trout's back is like the color of the stream's bottom. Sometimes the easiest way to find a rainbow trout is to look for its shadow.

When it is time to spawn, or lay eggs, rainbow trout look for streams that have clean, gravelly bottoms covered by riffles, stretches of water flowing rapidly downward over a rocky bottom.

Rainbow trout are native to those mountain streams of the West that empty into the Pacific Ocean from Alaska to Mexico. However, because they are such fine game fish and also can be easily transplanted to other waters, they have been introduced into lakes and streams across most of the United States and Canada. They are now found in many unpolluted eastern lakes and streams that have enough oxygen and a temperature lower than 75 degrees Fahrenheit (24 degrees Celsius).

The rainbow is named for the rosy band of scales that runs the length of its side. In some of their native waters along the West Coast, the fish migrate to the ocean, where they develop an overall gray color. This type of rainbow trout is called "steelhead." The steelhead's relatives include such fine game fish as salmon, the European brown trout, cutthroat, brook and lake trout.

Seagoing trout

There is no clear explanation why certain rainbow trout leave the stream where they were born and drift toward the sea, where some become steelheads. After several years of living in salt water, the steelhead swims back to the stream where it was hatched. Some biologists believe it finds the Pacific Coast by navigating with the stars, then locates its home stream by its sense of smell. It weighs about 10 pounds (four kilograms) at this point in its life.

In swimming upstream, the steelhead may have to climb waterfalls 10 feet (three meters) high. If it can't make it the first time, the fish continues to battle the water until it either succeeds or dies from exhaustion. It does not eat on this journey, and after spawning it returns to the sea. During its lifetime, a steelhead trout will make several of these spawning runs.

Laying eggs

Rainbow trout hunt for a place suitable for egg laying when the water becomes warm enough. Those that live in lakes may swim up streams to find the swift, clear water and gravel bottom that provide the necessary protection. The eggs must not be lost in the lake bottom silt, or fine particles of soil, where they cannot get enough oxygen. The female prepares a nest by fanning the site with her tail. Then she lays her eggs—anywhere from 200 to 20,000 at one time. The male stays close, and as the female pushes the eggs from her body, he fertilizes them by covering them with millions of living sperm.

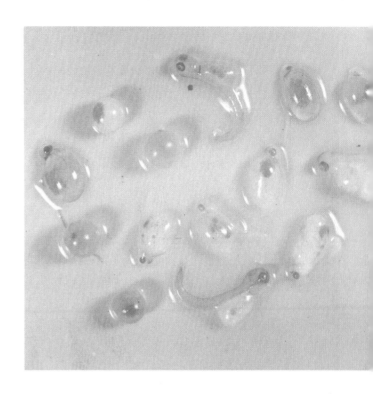

The eggs are round, about one-third inch (four-fifths centimeter) in diameter, and rather heavy for their size. The sperm swim to the eggs, and each bores through a rubbery shell to the interior. The spawning adults then leave the eggs to develop and grow by themselves. The female trout may lay eggs two or three times each spring.

The abundance of eggs is necessary, because there are many dangers facing a young trout. Heavy rains may bring silt, which causes eggs to decay. The eggs or the young trout may be eaten by snakes, birds and other fish.

If the egg falls into a protected spot, where the rushing water cannot wash it away and the gravel hides it from enemy eyes, its shell will become harder and the small fish will develop inside. The time required for the fertilized eggs to hatch depends on the temperature of the water. At 57 degrees Fahrenheit (14 degrees Celsius) it requires 22 days. In colder water, it takes more time.

That awkward age

When the egg finally hatches, the baby looks more like a fat worm than a fish. It cannot swim and gets its nourishment from an orange-colored sac, which is like a tiny egg yolk attached to its underside. In three or four weeks the food from the sac is gone, and gradually the tiny fish moves more and starts to swim. Still less than an inch (2½ centimeters) long, it can now move around and find its own food.

Growing up in a trout stream

At first, the tiny trout swims in open places among the gravel where it was hatched. As it grows larger, it moves to the quieter shallows at the sides of the stream, where it eats tiny animals called *zooplankton*. Toward summer, as the water gets warmer, the young fish begins to swim to the surface of the water for insects. By the age of five months, it is about two or three inches (five or eight centimeters) long. But only about one-tenth of all rainbow trout eggs laid live to reach this size.

Under ideal conditions and at a temperature of 63 degrees Fahrenheit (17 degrees Celsius) a rainbow can grow an inch (2½ centimeters) a month. However, these conditions are rare. It takes about two years for a trout to reach eight or nine inches (20 or 23 centimeters). Most rainbows caught are between six and 18 inches (15 and 45 centimeters). Steelheads of 18 to 20 pounds (6½ to 7½ kilograms) are not uncommon, and the weight of the largest rainbow ever caught with rod and reel is 37 pounds (14 kilograms). That fish was caught in a lake where there was plenty of food available for fast growth.

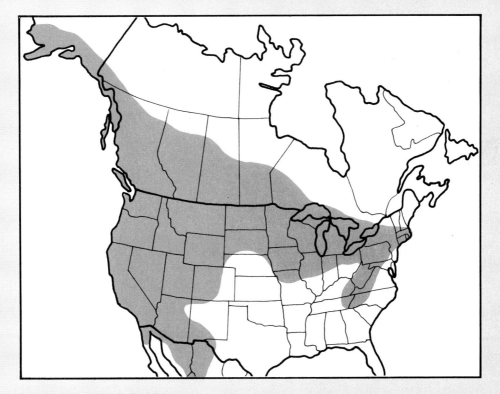

RAINBOW TROUT FACTS

Habitat: Native to cold, unpolluted waters of Pacific Coast mountain streams. Now introduced into unpolluted cool lakes and streams all over Canada and the United States.

Habits: Most active dawn and dusk.

Food: Insects, larvae, crustaceans, worms, small fish.

Size and Weight: Record weight, 37 pounds (17 kilograms). Average caught, 6-18 inches (15-45 centimeters).

Life Span: At least five-six years.

Locomotion: Swim; will leap out of water for insects.

Voice: None known.

The demand for sport fishing

Rainbow trout are favorites of fishermen because of their crafty nature and fighting spirit. To meet the demands of the growing number of fishermen, trout are now raised in protected structures called hatcheries. These fish are released in streams and lakes. Hatchery fish are not as lively fighters as streambred fish until they live wild a while.

In recent years, fish managers have also been trying to preserve and maintain unpolluted streams with gravelly bottoms for spawning. Deep pools and overhanging banks to provide feeding areas and places to hide have also been dug.

47

The Bighorn Sheep

Can a 300 pound (135 kilogram) animal walk without falling on high, steep, rugged mountain trails only two inches (five centimeters) wide? Yes. Bighorn sheep do it every day of their lives. They are such wonderful leapers and climbers that wolves, coyotes, wolverines, lynxes, bobcats, cougars and bears find it nearly impossible to catch them. Hard, double-shelled hooves and soft, cushiony pads in the middle make it easy for bighorns to travel, even on the slipperiest rock surfaces.

The bighorn feeds mainly on grasses, but also eats sedges, herbs and buds of various trees. In winter, the sheep may have to dig through snow for food. With powerful strokes of its front legs, it sends the snow flying backward. At times, it may paw at the rate of 1,800 strokes per hour to get at snow-covered plants.

Among bighorns, as in all members of the sheep family, adult males are called rams, adult females are ewes, and the young are lambs. During most of the year, the rams stay in separate herds. In the fall, they join the females for the breeding season, then separate again into their bachelor herds.

Rams have impressive horns, which curve around in corkscrew fashion. The horns are permanent and continue to grow throughout the bighorn's life. They weigh 20 to 30 pounds (nine to 14 kilograms) each, sometimes equaling the total weight of all the bones in the ram's body.

Ewes, too, have horns. Theirs, however, are small and curve slightly backward.

Summers on high

A few bighorns spend their entire lives within a one mile (2.5 square kilometer) area. Most, however, spend their summers high in the mountains and their winters in the lowlands. Traveling in a zig-zag pattern along the ridges, bighorns follow traditional migration routes by following the adults.

Summer ranges may be on grassy slopes or alpine meadows as high as 10,000 feet (three kilometers). Winter ranges are at much lower levels, perhaps only 2,000 to 3,000 feet (600 to 900 meters). For the winter months, bighorns choose a slope facing south to catch as much of the sun's warmth as possible. A good wintering slope will offer a supply of food and will be kept clear of snow by wind and sun.

The sheep begin their migration from summer to winter ranges after the first heavy snowfall, usually in October. As they start moving down the mountain, the urge to breed also stirs.

Giant headaches

During most of the year, the rams have been challenging each other to head-butting duels, to see which are the mightiest. These are the rams that will mate with most of the ewes.

Sometimes, when the breeding season arrives, there is still some question about who is the leader. Usually, it is the strong-est ram with the largest horns. But he is often challenged. The routine is always the same. Pretending not to notice each other, the two rams nibble on grass, inching a little closer with each mouthful. When they are within fighting distance, both rams suddenly rear up on their hind legs at exactly the same moment. Then, dropping down on all fours, they charge each other at full speed. At the last instant, they snap their heads down. Their massive horns meet with a thundering crash that can be heard more than a mile (1.6 kilometers) away. Dazed, they bounce back and stand still for a few seconds. Then, they go at it again.

Sometimes the loser accepts defeat after only a few clashes. Other times the battles go on for hours. Rams have been seen smashing their horns together as many as 48 times in one day. Though these fights are serious and may be long and tiring, severe injuries are rare. Generally, cracked horns and broken noses are the only damages.

Nature has provided bighorn rams with head protection that is more effective than the best football helmet. Their double-layered skulls and thick facial hide allow them to withstand the tremendous force of the horn-clashing without injuring their heads or brains.

Mother raises the young

When the breeding season is over, the rams return to their bachelor herds. The raising and protection of the young is left to the ewes.

The lambs are born in May, while the bighorns are still on their wintering grounds. When a ewe is ready to give birth, she looks for a steep, well-hidden rocky cliff that can usually be approached from only one direction. This provides the best protection against enemies.

Bighorn ewes usually have one lamb, although a few have been known to give birth to twins. The baby is born with a covering of woolly, brownish-gray fuzz. It weighs eight to nine pounds (three to 3½ kilograms) and stands only 10 or 11 inches (25 or 28 centimeters) high at the shoulder.

Within a few hours, the lamb stands on wobbly legs to reach its mother's milk. For the first week, the ewe keeps the youngster in its cliffside nursery. During this time, the lamb learns to run and begins to nibble on grass and tender plants. At the end of the week, the ewe leads her lamb back to the main herd.

No more vast herds

Like so many North American mammals, the bighorn sheep came to our continent across the Bering Land Bridge, which once connected Siberia and Alaska. They spread southward, well into Mexico, and grazed by the thousands throughout their range. The bighorn was one of the most plentiful animals found by early explorers.

With the settlement of the West, the bighorn began to disappear. Market hunters killed great numbers to sell for meat. Domestic sheep and cattle, however, created the most serious problems for the bighorns. Bighorns and livestock eat the same kinds of food. There was not enough grass for all. Loss of grasslands to overgrazing, highways, human settlements and recreation areas has greatly reduced the range of the bighorn. Today, the vast herds that once blanketed our Rocky Mountain states have shrunk to about 10 percent of their original numbers. No one knows exactly how many bighorns are alive today, but each year fewer and fewer are seen. Though it took nearly 2½ million years for the bighorns to spread across western North America, it took human beings less than a century to nearly wipe them out.

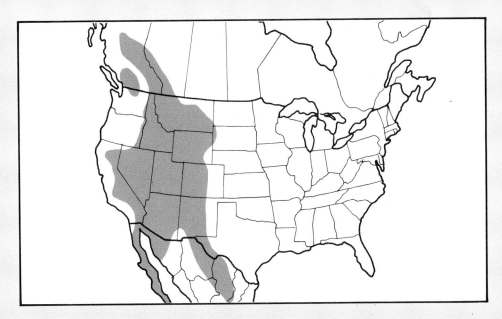

ROCKY MOUNTAIN BIGHORN SHEEP FACTS
Habitat: Western mountain slopes, usually in or near rugged areas.
Habits: Active during day. Herds usually separate according to sex, except during breeding season.
Food: Mostly grasses. In winter, will eat twigs and buds. Fond of mineral and salt licks.
Size and Weight: Rams stand three feet (one meter) high at shoulder; 4½-6 feet (1½-2 meters) in length; weight 200-300 pounds (90-135 kilograms). Ewes are at least one-quarter smaller than rams.
Life Span: Ten to 16 years in the wild. One ram was known to live for more than 20 years.
Locomotion: Usually walk. Will trot if disturbed. Seldom gallop, but have been clocked at over 35 miles (56 kilometers) per hour. Can cover 17 feet (five meters) in a leap. Easily can go up and down steep slopes at full speed. Strong swimmers.
Voice: Lambs bleat like barnyard lambs. Adults snort, grunt, grind their teeth and bleat.

Help for the bighorn

To save the few remaining herds, groups of bighorns are trapped by biologists and taken to areas where bighorns once lived. Here the animals are released, unharmed. In some cases, the new herds have had problems finding adequate protection and isolation. In other areas, they are doing well. Thirty years ago, there were no bighorns in the state of Washington. Today, there are more than 400, thanks to a successful "trap-and-transfer" program. In 1963, 38 bighorns were brought into southwestern Idaho. Since then, the herd has increased to nearly 150 animals.

Transfers may help to save the bighorn from extinction. Moving the sheep to new areas expands the animals' range and establishes new flocks.

The Clark's Nutcracker

People who drive to wayside stops and pull-offs along high mountain roads in the West need no introduction to the Clark's nutcracker. After years of complete protection in national parks, this gray bird with black and white wings has become a fearless roadside beggar. It will perch on the head and hands of any person who offers peanuts and other tidbits. Although not quite so boldly as some other jays, the nutcracker also scavenges for food scraps around mountain campgrounds. It shares the title of "camp robber" with its close relative, the gray jay, or "whiskey jack."

Like Lewis' woodpecker, Clark's nutcracker was named for one of the leaders of the Lewis and Clark expedition. The two explorers discovered both birds while journeying through the West in 1804-06. Captain William Clark described the nutcracker as "a new species of woodpecker," for the nutcracker flies like a woodpecker. But Captain Clark was wrong. The nutcracker is a member of the crow family and is closely related to the jays. It walks and hops like a crow, is noisy like a jay and has inherited the family's habit of robbing smaller birds of eggs and young. An old scientific name for this bird is *Picicorvus*, or "woodpecker-crow."

One scientist studying the voice of this bird heard it give nine different calls. He described all of them as "harsh, grating and unpleasant." But despite its reputation as a noisy bird, the nutcracker remains silent near its nest, probably to avoid attracting enemies.

Nutcrackers hide food

A nutcracker uses its long, pointed bill as a crowbar to pry open evergreen cones or as an axe to hammer them open to get the seeds inside.

The bird often hides seeds in the ground, where they remain until needed for food in the winter. A scientist who examined two female nutcrackers that had been shot while carrying seeds to a hiding place found 72 pinyon pine seeds in one's throat and 65 seeds in the other's.

Do birds remember these hiding places? Of all the different kinds of birds that store food for future use, Clark's nutcracker seems to have the best memory. It can find food buried several months before—even after snow has blanketed the hiding place.

These birds usually live in one area year-round. In the fall of the year they are numerous where nuts, especially pinyon nuts, are abundant. But in certain winters the birds are forced to leave their homes because there is not enough food for them to survive. When food grows scarce, huge flocks of nutcrackers migrate into other regions where they are not normally seen.

Nest in snow country

To find the nest of the Clark's nutcracker, you may have to begin looking as early as March or April and travel on snowshoes over deep mountain drifts. The nest is usually built six to 80 feet (two to 24 meters) above the ground on a horizontal limb of an evergreen, where it is sheltered from the cold winds.

Both birds share in gathering material for their nest, but the female is more active in arranging and adjusting the fresh material. The male, arriving with a twig in his bill, will pass it to his mate.

The outside of the nest is made of sticks and twigs. In one nest in Montana, 247 dead Douglas fir twigs were counted. Most twigs were eight or nine inches (20 or 23 centimeters) long, but some measured nearly 12 inches (30 centimeters). The nest's deep, cup-shaped lining and thick walls are made of dried

grass and fine strips of inner tree bark.

Three, and sometimes two or four, brown-spotted, greenish eggs are laid. It takes 18 days for the eggs to hatch. The female spends more time sitting on the eggs than her mate, but both birds take turns. The male has a brood patch on its breast, a bare spot where the eggs can touch the warmth of the body. Probably, this is one reason that nutcracker eggs do not freeze in nests built when there is still snow on the ground. In very cold weather, eggs and young are rarely left uncovered, and a nutcracker sitting on its nest usually refuses to fly away when disturbed. Stories are told about people actually picking up the sitting bird. When the male is not incubating, or sitting on the eggs, he patrols his territory and is alert to any other nutcrackers that may come near. A strange nutcracker is usually attacked and driven away. The female nutcracker seems to leave the defense of the home grounds to her mate. Birds other than rival nutcrackers are not bothered by either of the parent birds.

The babies stay in the nest for almost three weeks. After they leave the nest they are fed by their parents until they are able to find their own food.

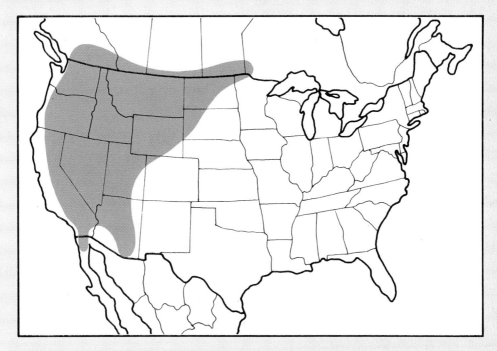

CLARK'S NUTCRACKER FACTS

Habitat: In stands of juniper, ponderosa pine, larch in high mountain ranges of the West.

Habits: Non-migratory, but flocks sometimes move into new area when winter food is scarce. Nests early, usually when snow is still on ground.

Food: Nuts and seeds, especially pinyon and other pine seeds; insects. Will also accept a variety of foods offered by campers and roadside tourists.

Size: Twelve to 13 inches (30-33 centimeters) long (larger than a robin).

Life Span: Probably three-five years.

Locomotion: Walks and hops like crow. Flight is up and down (woodpecker-like).

Voice: Noisy, like its close relative, the jay; generally harsh, grating and unpleasant. Silent near nest.

What Can YOU Do?

M an has found it difficult to tame the mountains. Because they are high and have long, tough winters man has been slow to build roads and to establish homes there. This has made it easier for mountain wildlife to survive. But even in the rugged peaks many kinds of wildlife are under pressure. Man is finding more ways to develop mountain lands. Highways are expanding. Ski slopes, villages, timber and mining operations are moving into the mountains.

What is the solution?

1. Congress is considering expansion of wilderness areas. Most of these are in the mountains. Natural areas will be preserved, and that will help wildlife. There will be no roads or public campgrounds in these areas. Write your Congressman telling him you want the wilderness preserved.

2. Learn all you can about the wildlife that lives in the mountains. Find out how it is suited for living in remote and rugged areas. Write to the mountain states to find out what their conservation departments are doing to help wildlife. Write to the Secretary of the Interior and the Chief of the United States Forest Service in Washington, D.C. 20240, and find out what they are doing to assure that mountain wildlife will have enough living space to remain healthy.

3. We have heard much about the energy crisis. We also know that energy resources are abundant in the mountains of North America. There is coal in the Appalachians; there is coal and shale oil in the Rockies. The problem is learning how to get the oil out of the rocks. Study the valuable minerals found in both mountain ranges, and try to figure what effect the development of these minerals will have on wildlife. We must help the wildlife while we are mining the energy.

4. Be informed about mountain wildlife and habitat. Write: American Alpine Club, 113 East 90th Street, New York, NY 10028; Appalachian Mountain Club, 5 Joy Street, Boston, MA 02108; Appalachian Trail Conference, Inc., P.O. Box 236, Harpers Ferry, WV 25425; Rocky Mountain Center on Environment, 1115 Grant Street, Denver, CO 80203; Bureau of Outdoor Recreation, Washington, D.C. 20240.

Projects you can do

Plant an alpine garden
Learn what kinds of flowers grow in the alpine meadows above the tree line. Send for seeds or plants and grow an alpine garden in your school yard or in a big box in your classroom.

Make a relief map of mountains
Study the two major mountain ranges in North America (Rockies and Appalachians). Then build a papier-mache map of North America showing the relative height of each range of mountains compared to the prairies, desert and Arctic.

Mountain wildlife scrapbook
Cut out photographs and paintings of mountain wildlife from magazines and other publications and make a class scrapbook. Write student comments or captions under the pictures telling how each creature is able to live in the mountains.

Trip across trail ridge
If you do not live close to Rocky Mountain National Park, take an imaginary trip across Trail Ridge Road. This road through the park is one of the highest and most dramatic roads in the world. Write to park headquarters in Estes Park, Colorado 80517, for literature on the road. Then, pretend you are in a bus driving across the road. How does the forest change as you climb higher? What does it look like above the tree line? What kind of wildlife do you see in each region as you get higher and higher? Why is it called Trail Ridge? Why does the highest point look like the Arctic?

While you're in the mountains...

There are many things each of us can do to help preserve America's beautiful mountains. The first is to know what to do and what not to do.

Stay on mountain trails
Mountain plants and grasses are very fragile. A single footprint on alpine tundra may be enough to start erosion. Don't take shortcuts. Stay on marked trails.

Weather can change rapidly
Mountains have sudden, violent storms. Weather can change from sun to rain, hail or even snow in minutes. Carry warm clothing and be prepared.

Be careful with fires
Scrape away the layer of dead leaves, called "duff," and build your fire on bare mineral soil. Burn only dead wood you find on the ground. Better yet, carry a small backpacker's stove that uses its own fuel.

Don't be a litterbug
Don't leave garbage and other trash in mountains—carry it out. A can left on a mountain slope will be there years later.

Protect wintering wildlife
Do not disturb animals during the winter. Winter is a time of great stress for all mountain wildlife.

Leave baby wildlife alone
If you come across a baby animal leave it alone. Chances are the mother is hiding nearby. Besides, there's little chance that the creature will survive if you attempt to care for it at home.

TEXT AND DESIGN: Market Communications, Inc.
Cliff Ganschow, chairman
H. Lee Schwanz, president
Glenn Helgeland, editorial director
Al Jacobs, art director
George Harrison, senior editor
Hal H. Harrison, Kit Harrison
and Valjean McLenighan, associate editors
Cheryl S. Bernard, Cynthia Swanson, Kathy
Sieja, Nanci Krajcir and Nancy Branson,
editorial assistants
Faith Williams, Robin Berens and Maureen Maguire,
production staff

PHOTOGRAPHERS: F. Eugene Hester: Front Cover, Page 24
Grant Heilman: Title Page, Pages 3, 46, 51, 52
Rollie Ostermick: Back Cover, Pages 8, 10, 13, 14
Leonard Lee Rue III: Page 11
Leonard Lee Rue III (Bruce Coleman, Inc.): Pages 20, 28, 33, 50
Rolf O. Peterson: Page 12
Bob Calhoun (Bruce Coleman, Inc.): Page 16
Joseph Van Wormer (Bruce Coleman, Inc.): Pages 18, 42, 44, 58-59
Hal Harrison (Grant Heilman): Page 19
Larry R. Ditto (Bruce Coleman, Inc.): Page 22
George H. Harrison: Pages 25, 36, 39, 56
John Shaw (Bruce Coleman, Inc.): Page 26
Tom Brakefield (Bruce Coleman, Inc.): Pages 27, 40, 48
Erwin A. Bauer: Page 30
K. W. Fink (Bruce Coleman, Inc.): Page 32
Craig D. Larson (Bruce Coleman, Inc.): Page 34
Vic Beunza (Bruce Coleman, Inc.): Page 38
Jeff Foott (Bruce Coleman, Inc.): Page 45
Harry Engels (Bruce Coleman, Inc.): Pages 54, 57

ART: Jay Blair: Pages 6-7